Remineralization

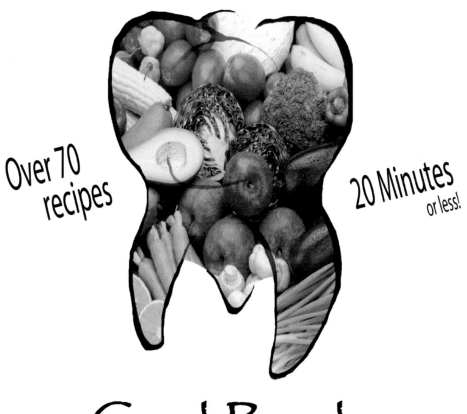

Over 70 recipes

20 Minutes or less!

CookBook

Life is what you make of it,
so make it taste good!

Written By

Jarrod Hebert

A special thanks
to my wonderful Family and Friends

I grew up with a loving family whose focus has always been on healthy living. They have all been very supportive throughout my life, for which I will always be grateful. Friends are there for you when you need them, my friends have been there for me always. You all know who you are, yes, you too! Thank you!

My Grandmother

Three Generations of health start with this incredible woman and the amazing man she married, who will be in our hearts always. She spent her days working with a natural health practitioner as a nutritionist and an awesome masseuse. Learning both practiced medicine and homeopathic remedies to heal ailments. This wasn't just a job for her, it was a passion as well as a way of life.

My Mother

A hero when I was afraid, my strength when I was weak, the woman who instilled upon me the greatness of our Lord, one of the best moms someone could ask for. She taught me that health is a duty, life is a gift.

"Listen with care to Me, eat what is good and let your soul delight itself in abundance"

Isaiah 55:2

My Father

My Father taught me how to be a man with love in his heart and honor in his soul. He would always make the hard sacrifices for his family. Dad, I have and will always look up to you, even though I'm a little taller.

This book is dedicated to the love of my life,

without whom, none of this would be possible.

She has always believed in me and the dreams I have.

Even the dreams that seem so far away. Thank you!

My Love,

Rae

Contents

Introduction

Congratulations on your first step to a healthy smile and improved overall health. If you just recently bought this book then you may already know the amazing benefits of remineralization. Maybe you've never heard of remineralization and received this book from a loved one. If that's the case, then prepare to have your beliefs in oral care changed forever. Even though this is a cookbook, you will find it has a lot of invaluable information that will get you started on your new adventure. Let's face it, eating better is always a good way to improve your health. But yes… it can improve the health of your teeth as well.

How do you keep your mouth healthy and clean? Well, if you're like most, you limit your sweets, brush twice a day with fluoride based products, floss a few times a week and use mouthwash to assist with freshness that brushing doesn't take care of.

Does this sound about right?

With all that you do caring for your teeth, just when you think you're good, the dentist hits you with the dreaded news, you have a cavity or worse, you need major dental work! After trying to figure out a way to cover the estimated charges given by the dentist and crying for a few hours, you wipe the tears and reflect back on your life.

How could this happen?

I follow the standards given by the American Dental Association "brush twice a day and floss once a day". But maybe that wasn't enough. Throughout the week I have been known to sneak in a few sweets, pastries and the occasional soda. Did I eat too much candy? Is it my beloved pastries? Maybe it's my second wind junk food drawer I have stashed at work?

Your dentist will likely tell you that it's all those corrosive, sugary foods you're eating. They'll probably show you how to brush the correct way and maybe suggest using a different toothpaste. And on the way out of the dentist, the hygienist, the secretary and even the janitor will remind you of the most important thing of all, floss, floss, floss!

Have you ever heard "If you don't brush within ten minutes of eating anything sugary then brushing wouldn't help anyways, that it's too late? The sugar has done the damage?" Who can brush their teeth 20 times a day?

Maybe you think about switching your toothpaste or adding a different mouthwash, because obviously something isn't working. You'll diet for a few weeks, limiting all sugars, sodas, and any other guilty pleasures before you eventually put it behind you and go back to your usual "American diet", easy, fast and processed foods. Understandably so...we are all busy.

As with most things in life, there's more to the story. Not just to reduce the risk for cavities or gum disease, but to help heal decayed teeth and unhealthy gums. One thing to remember, good oral health isn't just for those who have good genetics or who have been lucky enough not to have any dental problems. It's for most anyone willing to try. Yes, heal decayed teeth and unhealthy gums!

A healthy smile is something that most of us can have. If you're willing to put in a little effort, you can reap the benefits of a remineralization program. It isn't just about cutting out all sweets and candy, although limiting sugar is definitely recommended and always a good idea. It's about a change in your diet for three weeks, taking a couple of natural supplements and using some natural remineralization tooth care products!

Sounds easy enough?

Okay, maybe changing your diet doesn't sound all that easy and certainly not a whole lot of fun. But...the outcome can be amazing and shorter than the latest fad diet many of us try multiple times a year, but this isn't really a diet, not really.

Curbing a habit!

Dietary changes can be one of the toughest things we do to torment ourselves. The whole point of this program is to naturally add nutrients that can to be easily absorbed into the body. Giving your body the tools needed to do what it does best, heal and repair.

One catch and it's the most important part. The tooth needs to be connected by a root to be treatable. Though the outside of your teeth can be treated with remineralization oral care products, the only way to heal from the inside out is for your tooth to be able to receive nutrients via the root. Simply put, no tooth with a root canal or damage to the root can reap the full benefits of remineralization. It will, on the other hand, be well taken care of from the outside with remineralization oral care.

Quest for Remineralization

My journey started two years ago with one of the worst pains I've had to endure in my life. A front tooth decided it wanted to make me suffer, and suffer I did. An old root canal failed, becoming infected. With it brought an abscess above the tooth. My face looked as though I went 5 rounds in the ring with a heavy weight champ. In case I didn't mention, I was in a lot of pain, like I have never felt before.

All this couldn't have come at the worst time, it just so happens my employer changed dental providers a few days before the abscess started. During this period of change, the Root Canal Retreatment I so desperately needed was denied. For financial reasons, I was forced to wait for approval through my new insurance company. It ended up taking about 4 months to get the work done. During this "waiting period", I was taking a course of antibiotics that seemed to not be working. So in desperation, I started looking for an alternative ways to reduce the swelling and maybe help naturally fight the infection.

A couple of days after starting my antibiotics, while killing time on a popular blog app, I randomly scrolled past a link that caught my eye. The posting was talking about remineralization and natural teeth whiting. So I clicked on it and found some cool information and a list of ingredients that were described as natural antibiotics, antimicrobials and some other cool anti-infection type stuff. I was amazed as I started to realize that this may just be what I was looking for.

After some research, I found something called oil pulling. Just a little coconut oil and a few drops of peppermint oil, you swish it around for about 15 minutes before "putting it" into the garbage. (If you put it down the drain you may eventually cause your sink to back up. As with most oils, it can become harder as it cools). The oil pulling was difficult at first, considering my whole face still hurt, but I pulled through, pun

intended. Who would have thought, after only one day, the pain seemed to be getting a little better, after a couple of days, the swelling had subsided. I can't tell you how great that was. Without knowing when I was going to get approval from my insurance for the Root Canal Retreatment, relief couldn't have come at a better time.

The thought of this still makes me smile!

What an awesome feeling this was, to find something that worked. At this point, I was only scratching the surface of what remineralization was, not yet realizing the magnitude of research I would find out there. As I dove deeper into remineralization, I realized this was more than just homeopathic toothpaste or organic mouthwashes, it is a whole oral care revolution, using only healthy food and natural products. This became my full time focus.

Finding what encouraged the body's natural remineralizing process was a little harder than I thought. With a surprising number of people currently using remineralization in their day to day lives, you can imagine the multitude of different opinions everyone had. I scoured the web in search of what seemed to be a 50,000 piece puzzle.

There was a common thread with people talking about nutrients that can promote the remineralization process. But most of the information was on what supplements to take, making up the difference in your diet with supplemental vitamins and minerals. When it comes to supplements, we are always searching for ones that have the best absorption rate and also cost effective. In my opinion, the best way to absorb nutrients is from a healthy diet, selecting the right food. Taking supplements seems very similar to flushing money down the toilet.

What I had difficulty finding was anything related to what foods help you receive the suggested nutrients. And when I was able to find anything related to remineralizing food, there wasn't any type of recipe for me to follow, let alone a cookbook. My thought was if you are asking me to "curb a habit" then someone had better be supplying me with a quick and easy recipe or even some type of food preparation options. I left the blogs, web pages, books I used for research empty handed.

My conclusion!

I felt it necessary to begin researching all the nutrients that promote the body's natural remineralizing process, finding what foods contained them and building recipes for a cookbook. My mother used to say that things can be tolerated in small doses, so I wanted to provide you with what I have found in the form of an easy to follow guide on remineralization, along with recipes to incorporate remineralizing foods into our daily lives.

Remineralization Diet

All the recipes in this cookbook are intended to give you the vitamins and minerals needed for an effective remineralization of your teeth and bones in the shortest amount of time. This includes the whiting of dark spots, healing of cavities and returning your gums to a natural, healthy pink color. I know, healing cavities is a bold statement, but why not give it a try and see what happens. You may be surprised how effective your body can be when given the right tools to do the job. If done properly and with no cheating, you could see a drastic change in your oral health within three weeks.

So, how does it work? It works by attacking from multiple fronts, cutting demineralizing foods from your diet, eating nutritious food, oral care products, supplements and a plan to keep your mouths PH level between 7.5 and 7.8. The first step is to eliminate foods with high levels of Phytic Acid and Oxalic Acid. These two acids have been shown to bind to nutrients, eventually passing through as toxins in your waste. Although there are other acids that rob your body of nutrients, Phytic Acid and Oxalic Acid can be the most damaging with Phytic Acid at the top of the list. Don't get me wrong, as with most bad things in the world, these acids can actually be beneficial for the body, acting very similar to a vitamin. But when it comes to remineralization, the bad outweigh the good.

Lacking in key nutrients, there is a strong risk of having brittle bones and tooth decay, as both will slowly die from the inside out. In teeth, not having the right balance of nutrients will lead to unhealthy dentin, sensitizing the pulp and gums. This leaves you vulnerable to decay and even infection. It can also affect the outside of the teeth. Striping away your strong enamel layers, which any dentist will tell you never grows back.

I have found that the "fact" that enamel never grows back is not entirely true. A full remineralization program can not only strengthen your enamel, it can also regain some of those lost layers. The only problem is that without consistently being on a remineralization regiment, you'll probably never fully regain all enamel lost due to mistreatment. But still, some is better than none.

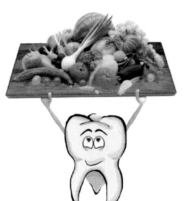

What's food got to do with it?

Let's get to the easier parts. The recipes in this book were hand selected because they contain foods that are high in the nutrients key to the remineralization process. Such as fat soluble vitamins A, D, E and K. And minerals like calcium, magnesium, phosphorus and gelatin. Also

activator X from grass-fed found in dairy products such as clarified butter or "ghee" (which I personally love). Because you'll be getting these nutrients from food, you shouldn't need supplements for the vitamins or minerals listed above. There are only two supplements recommended in this process, Fermented Cod Liver Oil and Vitamin butter.

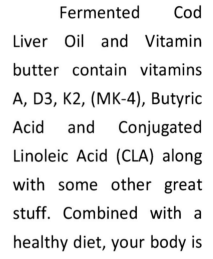

Fermented Cod Liver Oil and Vitamin butter contain vitamins A, D3, K2, (MK-4), Butyric Acid and Conjugated Linoleic Acid (CLA) along with some other great stuff. Combined with a healthy diet, your body is able to not only absorb nutrients better but it can to put them to work more efficiently. As you may already know, vitamins, acids, proteins and other nutrients always seem to work better in conjunction with a combination of nutrients, allowing for a harmonious balance.

Keeping your nutrients in the right balance can be a challenge to say the least. Let alone balancing the PH in your body or mouth. When the PH in your mouth falls below 7.0 for too long, the acidity will start to demineralize your teeth. This is most important after meals and drinks, as the average person's PH will drop to below 5.5 almost immediately. Left too long in this condition and you run the risk of tooth decay and gum disease. One thing to keep in mind is that your mouth is like a sensor for your stomach. It will signal to your brain telling it what enzymes are needed to break down your meal properly. To insure proper digestion, please make sure you wait anywhere between 20 to 40 minutes after a meal before using a PH restoring spray or mouthwash. But don't wait too long to restore your PH, especially after eating a highly acidic meal.

PH balancing Foods

Don't want to wait 20 minutes to balance your PH after a meal? Finish each meal with raw cauliflower, carrot, strawberry, mushrooms or cucumber. This rebalances your PH levels without interfering with digestion.

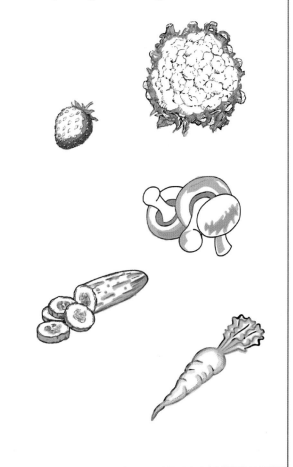

Three Week Remineralization Process

Remineralization is all about sticking with a process. This process can be very difficult with all the foods that need to be given up. Not just the cholate cake or candy bars, because as we all know, sweets are not great for teeth. It's the basic staples that can be found in most of our everyday diets, containing high levels of Phytic Acid. This includes grains, legumes and seeds, meaning ALL bread, pasta, nuts and beans. That's the hard part, the really hard part.

If you can get past those limitations, then the rest should be pretty easy. The good thing is that it's only for three weeks. After that, just limit the Phytic Acid by using methods such as sprouting, soaking, fermenting and other techniques to keep you mineralized until the next time you need a full remineralization. Which is recommended at least every 6 months or when needed, it's up to you.

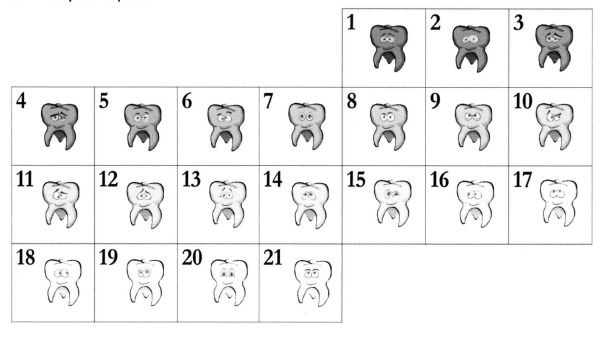

The Remineralization Process

For three weeks stay away from Phytic Acid and Oxalic Acid that can be found on the "Remineralization naughty list". This may be the most important part of the process.

1. Using the Remineralization Cookbook and foods from the "Good Food List"
   - *Eat fish at least twice a week*
   - *Use one bowl of bone broth daily, with food, as broth or alone*
   - *At least four servings of vegetables each day*
   - *3 to 4 meals a day with recipes from the Remineralization Cookbook*

2. Use Remineralizing oral care products daily
   - *Remineralizing Toothpaste*
   - *Mouthwash*
   - *Pre-Brushing Paste*
   - *Whitening Paste*
   - *Tooth Powder*

3. Supplements
   - *Fermented Cod Oil (twice a day)*
   - *Vitamin Butter Oil (once a day)*

4. PH balancing after meals. Rinse your mouth out with a PH balancing rinse or eat a PH balancing food to finish each meal. Either one is fine.

   A. Immediately finish each meal with raw, PH balancing foods
      - *Mushrooms*
      - *Strawberries*
      - *Cauliflower*
      - *Carrots*
      - *Cucumbers*

   B. Rinse at least 20 minutes after a meal to allow for proper digestion but no later than 40 minutes after a meal
      - *PH balancing mouthwash*
      - *Lemon water*
      - *Lime water*

Good Food List

Fruit

Apples (all varieties) ◇ Apricots

Bananas ◇ Blackberries

Cherries ◇ Exotic Fruit ◇ Star fruit

Quince ◇ Grapefruit ◇ Mango

Melon ◇ Pineapple ◇ Nectarines

Oranges ◇ Papaya ◇ Peaches

Pears ◇ Pomegranate

Strawberries ◇ Watermelon

Meat

Beef ◇ Fish ◇ Poultry ◇ Pork

Shellfish ◇ Lamb ◇ Most other meat

Vegetables

Anise/Fennel Root ◇ Artichoke

Arugula ◇ Asparagus ◇ Bell

Peppers ◇ Bok Choy ◇ Brussels

Sprouts ◇ Cucumber ◇ Cabbage

Cauliflower ◇ Garlic ◇ Green

Beans ◇ Greens (beet, mustard)

Jicama ◇ Kohlrabi ◇ Lettuce

Mushrooms ◇ Onion/Shallots

Rutabaga ◇ Rhubarb ◇ Snow

Peas ◇ Sugar Snap Peas

Zucchini ◇ Sprouts ◇ Tomato

Swiss Chard

Remineralization Naughty List

Phytic Acid

Nuts and Seeds

All Nuts ◇ All Seeds ◇ Peanuts Almonds ◇ Hazel nuts ◇ Brazil nuts Pecans ◇ Sesame seeds ◇ Poppy Seeds Sunflower seeds ◇ Cashews

Legumes and Grains

All Legumes ◇ All Grains ◇ Black beans ◇ Kidney beans ◇ Garbanzo beans ◇ Lima beans ◇ Brussel sprouts Whole wheat ◇ Oatmeal Buckwheat ◇ Amaranth

Oxalic Acid

Vegetables

Beets ◇ Sweet potatoes ◇ Dandelion greens ◇ Eggplant ◇ Kale Chives Broccoli ◇ Carrots ◇ Green Pepper Parsnips ◇ Potatoes ◇ Watercress Cassava ◇ Pumpkin ◇ Spinach Turnip greens ◇ Okra ◇ Collards Escarole ◇ Eeks ◇ Purslane ◇ Radish Celery

Fruits

Concord grapes ◇ Kiwi ◇ Lemon peel Figs ◇ Blueberries ◇ Raspberries Plums ◇ Tangerines ◇ Starfruit

Other Foods

Cinnamon ◇ Ginger ◇ Lettuce ◇ Soy products ◇ Chocolate ◇ Cocoa ◇ Tea Beer

Oral Care Ingredients

In the first section of The Remineralization Cookbook, I provided formulas for a few oral care products that are crucial for this process to work. I put together a powerful list of oral care products by pulling only the best ingredients found from all over the web. Don't be afraid to be your own mad scientist, mixing and matching different essential oils until you find what works best for you. It's a fun way to search for that perfect flavor. In the end, you'll enjoy the process that much more.

Below are some of the Remineralization ingredients that are great to work with.

Activated Charcoal ◦ Baking soda Bayberry ◦ Bentonite Clay Montmorillonite clay ◦ Borax Water ◦ Calcium Powder "Citrate" ◦ Cayenne Tincture Charcoal powder ◦ Cinnamon Oil ◦ Cinnamon powder ◦ Clove Oil ◦ Clove powder ◦ Coconut Oil ◦ Colloidal silver Diatomaceous Earth ◦ Echinacea Tincture ◦ Epsom salt ◦ Essential Oils ◦ Food grade peroxide Fresh Strawberry ◦ Lemon Essential oil ◦ Magnesium Powder ◦ Oak Gall (or 3X Oak Bark) ◦ Tincture ◦ Orange oil Peppermint Oil ◦ SEA SALT Himalayan ◦ Spearmint essential Oil ◦ Stevia ◦ Tea Tree Oil Trace minerals ◦ Turmeric Xylitol powder

Oral Care

Remineralizing
Toothpaste

Adjust the Essential oils to taste. The Lemon oil, Orange oil and Clover oil each can be removed for taste.

Ingredients:

- 1 tablespoon Baking Soda
- 1 tablespoon Bentonite Clay
- 4 tablespoons Calcium/Magnesium powder
- 1 tablespoon Sea Salt or Himalayan
- 2 tablespoon Stevia
- 3 tablespoons Xylitol powder
- 10-20 drops Cinnamon essential oil
- 10-30 drops Peppermint essential oil
- 15-30 drops Trace Minerals oil
- 3-20 drops Clover essential oil
- 3-15 drops Orange essential oil
- 3-10 drops Lemon essential oil
- 6 tablespoon Coconut oil
- 1/4 cup filtered water

How to use:

Use 2 to 6 time daily, mornings, nights and after meals.

Directions:

1. Place all dry ingredients in the food processor, Baking Soda, Bentonite Clay, Calcium, Sea Salt, Stevia and Xylitol powder and pulse until well mixed.
2. In a microwave safe bowl, add water.
3. Microwave on high for 30 seconds or until warm. (or warm on the stove)
4. Add Coconut oil to warm water, mix until Coconut oil has melted. Heat longer if necessary.
5. Add Cinnamon oil, Clover oil, Lemon oil, Orange oil, Peppermint oil and Trace Mineral oil to water and Coconut, Stir gently, about 30 seconds.
6. Slowly pour liquid in food processor pulsing as you go.
7. It should be a wet paste, add water if needed.
8. Pour the wet paste into a sealable glass container or separate into two containers and keep one in the refrigerator for up to 2 months.
9. The Coconut oil will firm as it cools, making it easier to add to your toothbrush.

Mouthwash
PH Balancing / Remineralizing

Adjust the oils to taste or feel free to add different oils to make it your own.

Ingredients:

- 2 teaspoons Calcium Carbonate / Magnesium powder
- 1 teaspoon Real Salt (Pink Himalayan Sea Salt)
- 1 tsp of Baking Soda
- 10 drops Concentrated Trace Minerals oil
- 10 drops Peppermint essential oil
- 3-7 drops Cinnamon essential oil
- 5 drops Spearmint essential oil
- 3-5 drops Lemon essential oil
- 1 ½ cups of filtered water

How to use:

Use mouthwash any time of day, after meals, acidic drink or just to freshen up. Rinse for 30 to 60 seconds.

Directions:

1. In a large glass mixing cup, stir dry ingredients together, Calcium/Magnesium, Salt and Baking Soda.
2. In a glass bottle (reused juice or apple cider vinegar bottle) mix, water, Trace Mineral oil, Peppermint oil, Lemon oil, Spearmint oil and Cinnamon oil.
3. Close lid and shake, about 20 seconds.
4. Using a funnel, add dry ingredients.
5. Close lid and shake, about 45-60 seconds.
6. Shake well before using.
7. Use as needed 1-2 times daily.
8. Rinse for 30-60 seconds.
9. Keep refrigerated for up to two weeks.

PH Balancing
Pre-Brushing Paste

A great way to bring your PH levels back after an acidic meal or drink.

Ingredients:

- 1 cup filtered water
- 1 teaspoon Baking Soda
- 20 drops Peppermint essential oil
- 5 teaspoons Xylitol powder

Directions:

1. In a large glass mixing cup, stir dry ingredients together, Baking Soda and Xylitol powder.
2. Add water and Peppermint oil.
3. Mix well into a paste, add Baking Soda or water to get desired results.
4. Use after acidic meals, drinks or just before regular bushing.
5. Keep refrigerated for up to two weeks.

How to use:

Use a gentle, soft brush to bring your protective PH levels back to normal.

Whitening
Paste

Use once or twice a week to bring out the natural beauty of your pearly whites.

Ingredients:

Whitener

- 2 tablespoon Charcoal powder
- 2 tablespoon Baking Soda
- 1 tablespoon Colloidal Silver
- 1 tablespoon Diatomaceous Earth
- 1 teaspoon Turmeric powder
- 1 tablespoon Epsom salt
- 3 tablespoon Coconut Oil
- 3 Fresh Strawberry's
- 10-15 drops Lemon essential oil
- ¼ cup food grade Peroxide
- ¼ cup Borax Water

Rinse

- 2 tablespoons Baking Soda
- 1 cup filtered water

How to use:

Use once to twice weekly as Diatomaceous Earth can be very abrasive. Brush teeth before whitening. Apply Whitener gently with a soft brush. Leave on teeth for 5-10 minutes. Rinse with Baking Soda water.

Directions:

Whitener

1. Place all dry ingredients, Baking Soda, Charcoal powder, Colloidal Silver, Diatomaceous Earth, Turmeric powder and Salt in the food processor and pulse until well mixed.
2. In a microwave safe bowl, add water.
3. Microwave on high for 30 seconds or until warm. (or warm on the stove)
4. Add Coconut oil to warm water, mix until Coconut oil has melted. Heat longer if necessary.
5. Add Lemon oil, Peroxide and Borax water to Coconut and water mixture, Stir gently, about 30 seconds.
6. Slowly pour liquid in food processor pulsing as you go.
7. It should be a paste, add water if needed.
8. Pour the wet paste into a sealable glass container or separate into two containers and keep one in the refrigerator for up to 2 months.
9. The Coconut oil will firm as it cools, making it easier to add to your toothbrush.

Rinse

1. Put water into a drinking glass.
2. Add Baking Soda and mix well, about 30 seconds.

Tooth Powder
PH Balancer

Use as a PH Balancer between meals or before brushing.

Ingredients:

- 1 tablespoon Activated Charcoal
- 1 tablespoon Baking Soda
- 4 tablespoon Bentonite Clay
- 4 tablespoon Calcium powder
- 1 tablespoon Cinnamon powder
- 1 tablespoon Clove powder
- 1 tablespoon Sea Salt or Himalayan
- 2 tablespoon Stevia
- 2 tablespoon Xylitol powder
- 2 tablespoon Peppermint Leaf powder

Directions:

1. In a glass jar, mix all the ingredients together, about 60 seconds.
2. To apply to toothbrush, dampen brush and dip into mixture.
3. Add a few drops of filtered water before brushing.

How to use:

Use after an acidic meal or after a good oil pulling to leave your mouth feeling fresh and clean.

Stock for the Soul

Bone broth is an inexpensive and flavorful way to add depth to your favorite dishes. Passed down through the generations, grandmas around the world have been boosting their family's immunity with nutritional stocks. Filled with minerals like calcium, magnesium, collagen and phosphorus, bone broth is an effective tool for the remineralization of teeth and bones.

Bone Broth

Bone Broth

Chicken Broth

Both broths take well over 20 minutes but are an essential tool in Remineralization. Make it once and freeze in small "one day" airtight containers for 1 to 4 months. Defrost and use in under 10 minutes!

Bone Broth
Grandmothers Stock

Prep Time: 10 mins   Total Time: 8 to 48 hours   Servings: 8 Cups

Ingredients:

- 4 pounds of bones from a healthy source, mix of
- marrow bones, bones with a little meat on them, oxtail and or short ribs
- 1 medium onion (optional)
- 1 garlic head (optional)
- 2 table spoons black peppercorns
- 1 teaspoon of kosher salt or sea salt
- 2 tablespoon Apple Cider Vinegar

Chef's Notes:

Bone broth can be made with just about any bone. When Roasting smaller bones, keep an eye on them and adjust the roast time accordingly.

Simmer times should be adjusted as well. See list below for cook times.

- Beef broth/stock: 48 hours

- Chicken or poultry broth/stock: 24 hours

- Fish broth: 8 hours

Directions:

1. Fill large pot with water and vinegar
2. Add bones to cold water
3. Let the bones blanch in cold water for 20 to 30 minutes
4. Pour water out and give the bones a quick rinse to remove vinegar, pat dry
5. Preheat oven to 450°F
6. Place dry bones on a roasting pan
7. Roast for 20 minutes then add onion and garlic
8. Roast for another 10 minutes
9. Add bones to a large pot or large crock pot
10. Fill with filtered water until all bones have just been covered
11. Bring to boil
12. Reduce heat to simmer, skimming the foam and fat from the surface for the first 2 to 3 hours, the better the bones, the less foam you will have
13. Simmer for at least 8 hours and as much as 48 hours, depending on your circumstances
14. Remove from heat and let cool until a lit steam is present
15. Remove all bones then strain out remaining solids
16. Let cool until safe to put into fridge or freezer
17. Put into storage containers
18. Cool in refrigerator until cold then remove thin layer of solidified fat on top
19. Place back in refrigerator or freeze for later use
20. Will keep up to 5 days in refrigerator and 4 months when frozen immediately after cool down

Chicken Stock
Simple base for soups

Prep Time: 30 mins   Total Time: 4 to 24 hours   Servings: 24

Ingredients:

- 5 pounds assorted chicken parts (necks, backs, legs and wings)
- 2 medium carrots, peeled and chopped into 2-inch lengths
- 2 celery stalks, chopped into 2-inch lengths
- 2 medium onions, peeled and cut into quarters
- 2 dried bay leaves
- 1 teaspoon whole black peppercorns

Directions:

1. Fill large pot with water and vinegar
2. Add bones to cold water
3. Let the bones blanch in cold water for 20 to 30 minutes
4. Pour water out and give the bones a quick rinse to remove vinegar, pat dry
5. Preheat oven to 400°F
6. Place dry bones on a roasting pan
7. Roast for 30 minutes
8. Place chicken in a 8-quart pot or crock pot with about 3 inches of room above
9. Add filtered water, should cover chicken by about 1 inch
10. Bring to a boil
11. Use a ladle to skim impurities and fat that rise to the top for the first 2 hours
12. Reduce heat to a simmer
13. Add vegetables, bay leaf, and peppercorns
14. Simmer for at least 4 hours and up to 24 hours
15. Pass stock through cheesecloth or cheesecloth lined sieve into a large pot
16. Skim off fat if using immediately, or let cool completely before transferring to airtight containers
17. Refrigerate at least 8 hours to allow the fat to accumulate at the top
18. Lift off and discard fat before using or storing stock
19. Keep refrigerated for up to 3 days or freeze for up to a month

5 Minute Recipes

Cucumber, Pineapple and Basil

Baked Artichoke Dip with Lemon and Feta

Kohlrabi Slaw

Tomato Salad with Olives and Lemon Zest

Cucumber
Pineapple and Basil

Prep Time: 5 mins   Total Time: 5 mins   Servings: 4

Ingredients:

- 1/2 cored pineapple, cut into 1/3-inch-thick half- or quarter-moons
- 1 small cucumber, halved lengthwise and thinly sliced on the bias
- 1/2 cup basil leaves (torn if large)
- 1 tablespoon extra-virgin olive oil
- 1/2 teaspoon coarse salt
- Freshly ground pepper

Directions:

1. Heat grill to high. Grill pineapple until grill marks appear, about 2 minutes per side. Let cool.
2. Toss with cucumber, basil, olive oil, and salt.
3. Sprinkle with pepper.

Cucumber, Pineapple and basil as a side dish for grilled shrimp. Oh yeah!

Baked Artichoke Dip
with Lemon and Feta

Ingredients:

- 12 ounces sheep's-milk feta
- ½ cup extra-virgin olive oil
- 1 can (13.75 ounces) quartered artichoke hearts, drained and cut in half
- 5 strips lemon zest
- 1 tablespoon packed fresh oregano leaves
- ¼ teaspoon red-pepper flakes

Directions:

1. Preheat oven to 350 degrees.
2. Place feta in middle of a 9-inch pie dish.
3. Pour oil over cheese, sprinkle remaining ingredients on and around it.
4. Cover with parchment-lined foil and bake until heated through, about 40 minutes.
5. Let cool slightly before serving with crackers or crostini.

Kohlrabi
Slaw

Ingredients:

- Kohlrabi, cut into matchsticks
- Apple, cut into matchsticks
- Olive oil
- Fresh lemon juice
- Salt and pepper

Directions:

1. Mix kohlrabi and apple matchsticks (both peeled or not) with olive oil and fresh lemon juice.
2. Season with salt and pepper.

Chef's Notes:

The outside layer of kohlrabi becomes tougher with age, so make sure to peel the skin before using. The younger plants should be tender so peeling may not be necessary.

Tomato Salad
with Olives and Lemon Zest

Ingredients:

- 2 pounds tomatoes (any variety)
- 1/4 cup mixed olives
- 1 lemon
- 2 tablespoons extra-virgin olive oil
- Coarse salt and ground pepper

Directions:

1. Arrange tomatoes and mixed olives on a serving plate.
2. Zest lemon over salad.
3. Drizzle with olive oil and season with salt and pepper.

10 Minute Recipes

Chorizo-Stuffed Mini Sweet Peppers

Zucchini, Bell Pepper, and Curry Paste

Asian Cabbage Slaw

Radicchio-Cabbage Slaw with Honey

Shredded Napa Cabbage Salad with Radishes Golden
Raisins, and Dijon Dressing

Asparagus and Cucumber Vinaigrette

Cucumber and Celery Salad with Tuna

Cucumber and Jicama Slaw

Fried Eggs with tomatoes and cheese

Carrot, Apple, and Fennel Slaw

Fennel and Orange Winter Salad

Orange, Fennel, and Olive Salad with Red-Pepper Flakes

Braised Green Beans

Mizuna Salad with Kohlrabi and Pomegranate Seeds

———

Sautéed Kohlrabi with Onions and Cream

———

Fennel and Smoked Salmon Salad

———

Pesto Snap Peas

———

Tomato and Avocado Salad

———

Tomato and Goat Cheese Salad with Basil Vinaigrette

———

Tomato and Beet Salad

———

Tomatoes with Ginger, Lemon, and Chili

———

Chorizo-Stuffed
Mini Sweet Peppers

Prep Time: 5 mins   Total Time: 10 mins   Servings: 4

Ingredients:

- 12 mini sweet peppers
- 12 slices dried chorizo or andouille (1/4-inch thick)

Directions:

1. Heat broiler, with rack in top position.
2. Make a long slit down three-fourths of the length of each pepper, leaving stem attached.
3. Stuff each pepper with 1 slice dried chorizo
4. Place on a rimmed baking sheet.
5. Turning peppers frequently, broil until peppers are blistered and browned on all sides, about 4 minutes.
6. Serve warm or at room temperature.

Bell Pepper, Zucchini
and Curry Paste

Prep Time: 5 mins   Total Time: 10 mins   Servings: 4

Ingredients:

- 1 tablespoon extra-virgin olive oil
- 1 large zucchini, sliced 1/3 inch thick on the bias
- 1 red bell pepper, sliced into 1/2-inch-thick strips
- 2 teaspoons Indian curry paste
- 1/2 teaspoon coarse salt

Directions:

1. Heat olive oil in a large nonstick skillet over high heat.
2. Sauté zucchini and bell pepper until tender, 5 to 6 minutes.
3. Stir in curry paste and salt.
4. Serve warm, cold, or at room temperature.

Pairs great with a baked, grilled or seared Salmon.

Asian
Cabbage Slaw

Ingredients:

- 2 tablespoons fresh lime juice
- 2 tablespoons rice vinegar
- 1 tablespoon vegetable oil
- 2 teaspoons sugar
- Salt
- 1/2 small head shredded Savoy or green cabbage
- 1 cup fresh cilantro leaves
- 4 scallions, cut into matchsticks
- 1 grated carrot
- 1/2 fresh jalapeno, minced

Directions:

1. In a large bowl, combine lime juice, rice vinegar, vegetable oil, and sugar.
2. Season with salt and whisk.
3. To dressing, add cabbage, cilantro leaves, scallions, carrot, and jalapeno, and toss to combine.

Radicchio-Cabbage Slaw with Honey

Ingredients:

- 3 tablespoons honey
- 3 tablespoons sherry vinegar
- 1 teaspoon coarse salt
- 1/3 cup extra-virgin olive oil
- Freshly ground pepper
- 1 medium head Napa cabbage (about 1 pound), halved lengthwise, then cut crosswise into 1/4-inch-thick strips
- 2 small heads radicchio (about 8 ounces), halved lengthwise, then cut crosswise into 1/4-inch-thick strips

Directions:

1. Whisk together honey, vinegar, and salt in a small bowl.
2. Add oil in a slow, steady stream, whisking until well blended.
3. Season with pepper.
4. Toss together cabbage and radicchio in a large bowl. Add dressing and toss to combine.
5. Cover, and refrigerate at least 5 minutes.
6. Just before serving, toss again.

Refrigerate any leftover slaw for up to 1 day in an airtight container.

Shredded Napa Cabbage Salad

with Radishes, Golden Raisins, and Dijon

Prep Time: 5 mins   Total Time: 10 mins   Servings: 6

Ingredients:

- 1/4 cup white-wine vinegar
- 2 tablespoons Dijon mustard, preferably whole grain
- 2 tablespoons sugar
- 1/2 small head Napa cabbage (about 12 ounces), cored and shredded (6 cups)
- 4 or 5 radishes, thinly sliced and cut into matchsticks
- 1/2 cup golden raisins
- 1 tablespoon thinly sliced fresh chives
- Coarse salt and freshly ground pepper

Directions:

1. Whisk together vinegar, mustard, and sugar.
2. Toss together cabbage, radishes, golden raisins, and chives.
3. Drizzle dressing over salad.
4. Season with salt and pepper.

Shopping for the perfect head of Napa cabbage is similar to shopping for lettuce, look for tender, crisp leaves.

 Asparagus
and Cucumber Vinaigrette

Prep Time: 10 mins   Total Time: 10 mins   Servings: 4

Ingredients:

- 1 bunch asparagus, tough ends removed, cut into 1 1/2-inch lengths
- 1 cucumber, peeled, quartered lengthwise, seeded, and cut into 1 1/2-inch strips
- 1 teaspoon red-wine vinegar
- 2 teaspoons olive oil
- Coarse salt and ground pepper

Directions:

1. Place a steamer basket in a saucepan filled with 1 inch water.
2. Bring to a boil.
3. Add asparagus, cover, and cook until crisp-tender, 3 to 5 minutes.
4. Rinse with cold water to stop the cooking.
5. In a bowl, combine asparagus, cucumber, vinegar, and oil.
6. Season with salt and pepper.

Cucumber
and Celery Salad with Tuna

Ingredients:

- 2 teaspoons poppy seeds
- 3 tablespoons rice vinegar
- 1 tablespoon sugar
- 2 tablespoons extra-virgin olive oil
- 2 cucumbers, halved lengthwise and cut into 1/4-inch half-moons (6 cups)
- 3 celery stalks, cut into 1/4-inch pieces, inner leaves reserved
- 2 cans (5 ounces each) solid white tuna in water, drained and flaked
- Coarse salt and ground pepper

Directions:

1. In a medium bowl, stir together poppy seeds, vinegar, sugar, and oil.
2. Add cucumbers, celery, and tuna.
3. Season with salt and pepper. Toss well to coat.
4. Sprinkle with celery leaves and serve immediately.

Want to add a little crunch without adding calories, cucumbers and celery will do the trick.

Cucumber
and Jicama Slaw

Prep Time: 10 mins   Total Time: 10 mins   Servings: 4

Ingredients:

- 1 English cucumber
- 1 small jicama
- 1 1/2 teaspoons honey
- 2 tablespoons fresh lime juice
- Coarse salt
- 1/4 teaspoon chili powder, such as ancho or chipotle

Directions:

1. Cut English cucumber into 3-inch lengths, then thinly slice lengthwise, avoiding center.
2. Cut slices into matchsticks.
3. Peel jicama and thinly slice.
4. Working with several slices at a time, stack and cut lengthwise into matchsticks.
5. In a bowl, toss jicama, cucumber, honey, and fresh lime juice until combined.
6. Season with salt and chili powder.

Cucumber
Ranch Dressing

Ingredients:

- 1 medium cucumber, peeled, halved lengthwise, seeded, and grated on the large holes of a box grater
- 1 tablespoon shallot, finely chopped
- ¾ cup sour cream
- ¼ cup low-fat buttermilk
- ¼ cup mayonnaise
- 3 ½ tablespoons (about 1 lemon) fresh lemon juice
- 1 ¼ teaspoons coarse salt
- Pinch of cayenne pepper
- 3 tablespoons fresh flat-leaf parsley, finely chopped
- 3 tablespoons fresh chives, finely chopped

Directions:

1. Stir together cucumber, shallot, sour cream, buttermilk, mayonnaise, lemon juice, salt, cayenne, parsley, and chives in a medium bowl.
2. Season with additional salt and cayenne, if desired, to taste.

Chef's Notes:

Refrigerate for up to 3 days in an airtight container.

Fried Eggs
with tomatoes and cheese

Prep Time: 5 mins   Total Time: 10 mins   Servings: 4

Ingredients:

- 1 teaspoons Ghee
- 3 large eggs
- Coarse salt and freshly ground pepper
- ½ cup mixed heirloom tomatoes, sliced
- ¼ cup sliced or finely grated extra-sharp cheddar cheese (1 ounce)

Directions:

1. Heat broiler.
2. Melt Ghee in an 8-inch nonstick ovenproof skillet over medium-high heat until foamy.
3. Crack eggs into skillet, and cook until whites are almost set, about 1 ½ minutes.
4. Remove from heat.
5. Season eggs with salt and pepper, and top with tomatoes, then cheese.
6. Broil until whites are set and cheese melts and is bubbling, about 1 minute.

Carrot, Apple
and Fennel Slaw

Ingredients:

- 1/2 cup plain nonfat yogurt
- 2 tablespoons white-wine vinegar
- 1/2 teaspoon celery seeds
- 1/4 teaspoon coarse salt
- 1 tablespoon freshly chopped tarragon
- 1 pound carrots, peeled and cut into 3-by-1/4-inch matchsticks
- 1 fennel bulb, cut into 3-by-1/4-inch matchsticks
- 1 Granny Smith apple, unpeeled, cored, and cut into 1/2-inch wedges

Directions:

1. Place the yogurt, white-wine vinegar, celery seeds, salt, and tarragon in a small bowl, and whisk to combine, set aside.
2. Place the carrot and fennel matchsticks and apple wedges in a medium bowl.
3. Add the reserved yogurt dressing, and toss to combine.
4. Serve.

Fennel and Orange
Winter Salad

Prep Time: 5 mins   Total Time: 10 mins   Servings: 12

Ingredients:

- 3 fennel bulbs, cut into 1-inch wedges
- 4 navel oranges, 3 cut into 1-inch wedges, 1 halved
- Extra-virgin olive oil, for drizzling
- Coarse salt and freshly ground pepper

Directions:

1. Arrange fennel and orange wedges on serving platters.
2. Squeeze orange halves over salad, and drizzle with oil.
3. Season with salt and pepper.

Orange, Fennel, and Olive Salad
with Red-Pepper Flakes

Prep Time: 5 mins   Total Time: 10 mins   Servings: 4

Ingredients:

- 1 fennel bulb, trimmed, reserved 1 to 2 tablespoons of fronds
- 2 tablespoons fresh lemon juice
- 2 oranges
- 1/4 cup small olives, such as Nicoise
- 2 tablespoons extra-virgin olive oil
- Coarse salt and ground pepper
- Red-pepper flakes

Directions:

1. Halve, core, and thinly slice fennel bulb (preferably on a mandolin).
2. In a bowl, toss fennel with lemon juice.
3. Slice away peel and pith of oranges and cut flesh into segments.
4. Add to bowl with fennel and stir in olives, reserved fennel fronds, and olive oil.
5. Season with salt, pepper, and red-pepper flakes.

Braised
Green Beans

Prep Time: 5 mins   Total Time: 10 mins   Servings: 4

Ingredients:

- 1 cup chicken broth
- 5 peeled cloves garlic
- 1 pound trimmed green beans
- 2 teaspoons fresh thyme leaves
- Salt and pepper
- Extra-virgin olive oil
- Lemon slices

Directions:

1. In a large skillet, bring chicken broth and garlic to a simmer over medium-high.
2. Add green beans and thyme, cover and cook until tender, about 8 minutes.
3. Season with salt and pepper, drizzle with olive oil, and serve with lemon slices.

Mizuna Salad

with Kohlrabi and Pomegranate Seeds

Prep Time: 10 mins   Total Time: 10 mins   Servings: 4

Ingredients:

- 2 large celery stalks
- 1 medium kohlrabi bulb (8 ounces), trimmed and peeled
- 1 small pomegranate
- 3 1/2 cups mizuna (3 ounces) or other tender, bitter salad greens such as arugula or dandelion
- 2 tablespoons champagne vinegar
- 1/8 teaspoon coarse salt
- 1/8 teaspoon freshly ground pepper
- 1/8 teaspoon sugar
- 1/2 teaspoon Dijon mustard
- 3 tablespoons extra-virgin olive oil

Directions:

1. Using a sharp knife, thinly slice the celery and kohlrabi.
2. Cut kohlrabi slices into 1/4-inch-wide strips.
3. Halve pomegranate and remove enough seeds to yield 1/2 cup (reserve remainder for another use).
4. Add seeds, celery, kohlrabi, and mizuna to a serving bowl.
5. Whisk together vinegar, salt, pepper, sugar, and mustard.
6. Whisking constantly, add oil in a slow, steady stream.
7. Whisk until emulsified.
8. Toss with salad.

Sautéed Kohlrabi
with Onions and Cream

Prep Time: 10 mins   Total Time: 10 mins   Servings: 4

Ingredients:

- 1 kohlrabi
- ½ white onion (Thinly sliced)
- 2 tablespoons of Ghee
- ¼ cup Heavy cream
- Salt and pepper to taste
- Grated nutmeg to taste

Directions:

1. Cut leaves off and set aside
2. Peeled and cube kohlrabi bulb (½ inch cubes)
3. Rinse and finely shred kohlrabi leaves
4. Cook kohlrabi cubes and onion in Ghee over medium-high heat until almost tender.
5. Stir in kohlrabi leaves, and cook until wilted.
6. Add heavy cream, and cook for a few seconds to reduce.
7. Season with salt, pepper, and nutmeg.

Chef's Notes:

To keep kohlrabi fresh, cut off the leaves and wrap them with a damp paper towel and store in a plastic bag. Should keep for 3 to 5 days in the refrigerator.

Rinse and dry the bulb with a paper tower and store in a plastic bag. Refrigerate for up to 4 weeks.

Great with chicken, pork chops, steak, or just about any meat.

Smoked Salmon
and Fennel Salad

Prep Time: 10 mins   Total Time: 10 mins   Servings: 4

Ingredients:

- 1 fennel bulb (about 8 ounces), thinly sliced
- 1/4 cup fennel fronds
- 1/2 teaspoon finely grated lemon zest
- 4 teaspoons lemon juice
- Pinch of Coarse salt and ground pepper
- 4 ounces thinly sliced smoked salmon
- 1 tablespoon extra-virgin olive oil

Directions:

1. In a medium bowl, toss fennel and fronds with lemon zest and juice.
2. Season with salt and pepper to taste.
3. Lay salmon on a serving plate
4. Top with fennel mixture, and drizzle with oil.
5. Serve right away or cover and chill for up to 1 hour.

Chef's Notes:

Not a fan of fennel? Use cucumber or celery instead. Or, if you like, add all three for a little more flare.

Don't have any salmon in the fringe? Try any smoked fish for similar results.

Pesto
Snap Peas

Prep Time: 5 mins   Total Time: 10 mins   Servings: 4

Ingredients:

- 1 pound snap peas
- 1/4 cup basil pesto
- Coarse salt and ground pepper

Directions:

1. In a large pot of boiling salted water, cook snap peas until crisp-tender and bright green, about 4 minutes.
2. Drain and toss with pesto.
3. Season with salt and pepper.

Tomato
and Avocado Salad

Ingredients:

- 2 pounds assorted tomatoes (any color), sliced or halved if small
- 1 avocado, halved, pitted, peeled, and sliced
- Extra-virgin olive oil
- Coarse salt and ground pepper

Directions:

1. On a large plate or platter, arrange tomatoes and avocado.
2. Drizzle with olive oil and season with salt and pepper.

Tomato and Goat-Cheese
Salad with Basil Vinaigrette

Prep Time: 10 mins   Total Time: 10 mins   Servings: 4

Ingredients:

- 1/2 cup packed fresh basil leaves, plus more for garnish
- 2 tablespoons olive oil
- 2 tablespoons white-wine vinegar
- Coarse salt and ground pepper
- 3 ounces fresh goat cheese
- 3 medium tomatoes, cored and sliced crosswise 1 inch thick

Directions:

1. In a blender, combine basil, oil, vinegar, and 1 tablespoon water.
2. Blend until smooth, 2 to 3 minutes.
3. Season vinaigrette with salt and pepper.
4. With dental floss or a warm knife (wiped clean after each slice), thinly slice cheese.
5. Arrange tomatoes and goat cheese on a serving plate, drizzle with dressing to taste.
6. Serve garnished with basil leaves.

Tomato
and Beet Salad

Ingredients:

- 1 pound scrubbed small beets
- 2 pounds tomatoes, preferably heirloom
- 1 pint cherry tomatoes
- 1/4 cup crumbled feta
- 1/4 cup fresh cilantro leaves
- 1/4 cup extra-virgin olive oil
- Salt and pepper

Directions:

1. Preheat oven to 400 degrees.
2. Seal beets in a foil packet.
3. Roast on a rimmed baking sheet until tender, 75 minutes.
4. When cool, rub beets with a paper towel to remove skins.
5. Slice large tomatoes, and halve cherry tomatoes, then arrange with beets on a platter.
6. Top with feta, cilantro, and olive oil.
7. Season with salt and pepper.

Chef's Notes:

Great With

Poached chicken, grilled steak or burgers

Tomatoes
with Ginger, Lemon, and Chili

Prep Time: 5 mins   Total Time: 10 mins   Servings: 4

Ingredients:

- 4 ripe tomatoes, cut into 1/2-inch wedges
- 1 small jalapeno or serrano chili, seeded and minced
- 2 tablespoons minced peeled fresh ginger
- Zest from 1 lemon, plus 2 tablespoons lemon juice
- 2 tablespoons extra-virgin olive oil
- Coarse salt and ground pepper

Directions:

1. In a large bowl, toss together tomatoes, jalapeno or serrano chili, ginger, lemon zest and juice, and olive oil.
2. Season with salt and pepper.

15 Minute Recipes

Arugula Salad with Figs and Radicchio

Green Salad with Buttermilk Dressing

Asparagus and Green Beans with Chili-Orange Oil

Asparagus with Creamy Mustard Sauce

Asparagus with Mint Butter

Beef, Snap Pea, and Asparagus Stir-Fry

Warm Brussels Sprout Salad

Cucumber Salad with Sour Cream and Dill Dressing

Classic Roasted Salsa

Creamy Zucchini and Ricotta Spread

Fennel, Escarole, and Radish Salad

Fried Green Beans

Green Beans Vinaigrette

Green Beans with Tomatoes, Olives, and Eggs

Mustard Greens and Onions

Mustard Greens and Sweet-Onion Sauté

Sautéed Shrimp with Arugula

Seared Salmon with Oranges and Fennel

Steamed Cod and Mixed Green Peas

Tilapia with Arugula, Capers, and Tomatoes

Grilled Zucchini with Buttermilk Basil Dressing

Arugula Salad
with Figs and Radicchio

Ingredients:

- 2 tablespoons olive oil
- 2 tablespoons balsamic vinegar
- Coarse salt and ground pepper
- 1 bunch (3 ounces) baby arugula
- 1 head radicchio, halved, cored, and cut into 1 1/2-inch-wide strips
- 1/2 pound ripe fresh figs (about 8), stemmed and quartered

Directions:

1. In a large bowl, whisk together oil and vinegar.
2. Season with salt and pepper.
3. Add arugula, radicchio and figs.
4. Toss to combine.

Chef's Notes:

Once a fig is ripe, they are highly perishable, so use them right away. You can also refrigerate a ripe fig to add a couple days of goodness.

Perfectly ripe figs are usually slightly cracked with a collection of sugar or honey at the stem

Green Salad
with Buttermilk Dressing

Prep Time: 15 mins   Total Time: 15 mins   Servings: 6

Ingredients:

- 1/4 cup reduced-fat sour cream
- 1/4 cup buttermilk
- 2 tablespoons cider vinegar
- 1 tablespoon honey
- 1 minced scallion
- Coarse salt and ground pepper
- 2 to 3 bunches arugula (1 pound), stems trimmed
- 4 heads Belgian endive, sliced crosswise 1 inch thick (4 cups)
- 2 tart green apples, cored and thinly sliced

Directions:

1. In a small bowl, whisk together sour cream, buttermilk, vinegar, honey, and scallion.
2. Season with salt and pepper.
3. In a large bowl, combine arugula, endive, and apples.
4. Toss with dressing.
5. Serve immediately.

The bitter flavor in Belgian endive is from "Intybin". Known to be a digestive aid, pain reliever and even a sedative.

Asparagus and Green Beans
with Chili-Orange Oil

Prep Time: 10 mins   Total Time: 15 mins   Servings: 8

Ingredients:

- 3 tablespoons extra-virgin olive oil
- 3 wide strips orange zest, plus 2 tablespoons orange juice
- 1/4 teaspoon red-pepper flakes
- Coarse salt and ground pepper
- 2 bunches asparagus (about a pound each), trimmed, cut into 2-inch lengths
- 1 pound green beans, trimmed, cut into 2-inch lengths
- 1/2 cup tightly packed fresh basil leaves

Directions:

1. In a small saucepan, bring oil, orange zest, and red-pepper flakes to a simmer over medium-high and cook 3 minutes.
2. Remove chili-orange oil from heat and set aside. (To store, refrigerate cooled oil in an airtight container, up to 3 days.)
3. Working in 2 batches, in a large pot of boiling salted water, cook asparagus and green beans separately until bright-green and crisp-tender, about 3 minutes.
4. Transfer to a colander and rinse with cool water to stop the cooking.
5. In a large skillet, heat 1 tablespoon chili-orange oil over high.
6. Add half the vegetables and cook, stirring often, until warmed through and tender, 3 minutes.
7. Stir in half the basil, season with salt and pepper, and transfer to a platter.
8. Repeat with 1 tablespoon oil and remaining vegetables and basil.
9. Drizzle with remaining oil and orange juice and serve immediately.

Asparagus

with Creamy Mustard Sauce

Ingredients:

- 2 tablespoons mayonnaise
- 1 tablespoon olive oil
- 1 tablespoon white-wine vinegar
- 1 teaspoon Dijon mustard
- Salt and pepper
- Steamed Asparagus

Directions:

1. In a bowl, stir together 2 tablespoons mayonnaise, 1 tablespoon olive oil, 1 tablespoon white-wine vinegar, and 1 teaspoon Dijon mustard.
2. Season with salt and pepper.
3. Drizzle over chilled Steamed Asparagus.

Asparagus
with Mint Butter

Prep Time: 15 mins   Total Time: 15 mins   Servings: 8

Ingredients:

Butter (MAKES 1/2 CUP)

- 1 stick unsalted butter, cut into small pieces
- 1/2 cup fresh mint, finely chopped
- Coarse salt and freshly ground pepper

Asparagus

- 1 pound trimmed asparagus
- Coarse salt
- Mint leaves (Garnish)

Chef's Notes:

Refrigerate any leftover Mint butter for up to a full week in an airtight container.

Directions:

Making the butter:

1. Add butter in a small saucepan over medium heat.
2. Add mint.
3. Add 1/2 teaspoon salt.
4. Add 1/4 teaspoon pepper.
5. Heat until just bubbling around edges.
6. Remove from heat.

Making the asparagus:

1. Cook asparagus in a pot of salted boiling water until bright green and tender, about 3 minutes.
2. Drain.
3. Drizzle a few tablespoons mint butter over asparagus, and toss gently to coat.
4. Garnish with mint leaves.

Beef, Snap Pea
and Asparagus Stir-Fry

Prep Time: 15 mins   Total Time: 15 mins   Servings: 4

Ingredients:

- 1 tablespoon soy sauce
- 1 teaspoon rice vinegar
- 1 teaspoon sugar
- ¾ pound boneless New York steak, thinly sliced
- Pinch of Coarse salt
- 1 tablespoon vegetable oil
- 1 bunch asparagus (14 ounces), cut into 2-inch lengths
- 6 ounces snap peas
- 1 garlic clove, minced
- 1 tablespoon peeled minced fresh ginger
- 1 teaspoon fresh lemon juice,
- 4 lemon wedges
- 2 tablespoons torn fresh basil leaves

Chef's Notes:

Don't have a wok? Leave the steak cooking longer on one side to get the perfect sear without overcooking it.

Directions:

1. In a small bowl, combine soy sauce, vinegar, and sugar.
2. Season steak with salt.
3. In a large skillet or wok, heat oil over high.
4. Cook steak, undisturbed, until brown on one side, about 2 minutes.
5. Flip and cook until cooked through, about 45 to 60 seconds.
6. Transfer to a bowl.
7. Add asparagus, snap peas, garlic, and ginger to skillet.
8. Cook, stirring constantly (add a little water if pan gets too dark), until vegetables are crisp-tender, about 4 minutes.
9. Add soy mixture and cook until fragrant, about 10 seconds.
10. Remove skillet from heat and stir in lemon juice and basil.
11. Toss steak with vegetables.
12. Serve with lemon wedges if desired.

Warm Brussels Sprout Salad

Ingredients:

- 2 tablespoons extra-virgin olive oil
- 3/4 pound Brussels sprouts, trimmed and shredded
- Coarse salt and ground pepper
- 3 tablespoons fresh lemon juice
- 1/4 cup grated pecorino cheese (1/2 ounce)

Chef's Notes:

Shredding Brussels sprouts is as simple as cutting in half long ways, then chopping from the top to the base.

Directions:

1. In a large skillet, heat 1 tablespoon oil over medium-high.
2. Add Brussels sprouts.
3. Season with salt and pepper and cook, tossing often, until bright green and slightly wilted, about 3 minutes.
4. Add lemon juice and transfer to a large bowl.
5. Add cheese and 1 tablespoon oil, toss well to combine and season with salt and pepper.

Cucumber Salad
with Sour Cream and Dill Dressing

Prep Time: 15 mins   Total Time: 15 mins   Servings: 4

Ingredients:

- 1/2 cup reduced-fat sour cream
- 2 tablespoons fresh lemon juice (from 1 lemon)
- 2 tablespoons chopped fresh dill, plus more for garnish (optional)
- Coarse salt and ground pepper
- 4 to 6 Kirby cucumbers (about 1 pound), halved lengthwise and thinly sliced crosswise

Directions:

1. In a medium bowl, combine sour cream, lemon juice, and dill.
2. Season with salt and pepper, and whisk well to combine.
3. Add cucumbers, and toss to coat.
4. Garnish with more dill, if desired.
5. Serve, or refrigerate, covered, up to 4 hours.

Classic
Roasted Salsa

Ingredients:

- 2 large tomatoes (1 ½ pounds)
- 1 medium white onion, halved
- 3 jalapenos
- 3 garlic cloves, unpeeled
- 3 tablespoons fresh lime juice (from 2 limes)
- Coarse salt and ground pepper
- ¼ cup chopped fresh cilantro

Chef's Notes:

Want a little less heat, remove the seeds from the jalapenos or start with ½ a jalapeno and add more to taste.

To turn this into a green salsa, replace tomatoes with tomatillos and reduce the lime juice to 1 tablespoon or to taste.

Directions:

1. Heat broiler, with rack in top position.
2. Place tomatoes, onion, jalapenos, and garlic in a single layer on a rimmed baking sheet.
3. Broil until vegetables are blistered and slightly softened, rotating sheet and flipping vegetables frequently, 6 to 8 minutes (garlic may need to be removed earlier, if it is browning too quickly).
4. Discard garlic skins.
5. In a food processor, pulse garlic and vegetables until coarsely pureed.
6. Add lime juice, season with salt and pepper, and pulse to combine.
7. Transfer salsa to a bowl and stir in cilantro.
8. Refrigerate up to 3 days in an airtight container or freeze for up to 3 months.

Creamy Zucchini
and Ricotta Spread

Ingredients:

- 1 teaspoon extra-virgin olive oil
- 1 medium zucchini, grated on the large holes of a box grater
- 1 garlic clove, minced
- ½ teaspoon fresh thyme leaves
- Coarse salt and ground pepper
- ½ cup ricotta
- 1 tablespoon lemon zest
- 2 teaspoon lemon juice

Directions:

1. In a medium nonstick skillet, heat olive oil over medium-high.
2. Add zucchini, garlic, and thyme, season with salt and pepper.
3. Cook, stirring occasionally, until zucchini is tender and golden brown in spots, about 5 minutes.
4. Transfer to a medium bowl and let cool to room temperature (or refrigerate, up to overnight, bring to room temperature before continuing).
5. Add ricotta, lemon zest, and lemon juice, and stir to combine.
6. Season with salt and pepper.

Fennel, Escarole
and Radish Salad

Ingredients:

- 1 head escarole, cut crosswise into 2-inch-wide ribbons
- 1 bunch small or medium radishes, thinly sliced
- 1 fennel bulb, thinly sliced crosswise, fronds reserved
- 1 tablespoon extra-virgin olive oil
- 2 teaspoons champagne vinegar
- Coarse salt and freshly ground pepper

Directions:

1. Toss together escarole, radishes, and fennel bulb in a large bowl.
2. Drizzle oil and vinegar on top, and season with salt and pepper.
3. Gently toss.
4. Garnish with fennel fronds.

The bitterness of the Escarole plays well with radishes.

Fried
Green Beans

Prep Time: 5 mins   Total Time: 15 mins   Servings: 4

Ingredients:

- Grapeseed oil, for frying
- 4 egg whites
- 3 cups flour
- 2 3/4 cups plus 2 tablespoons club soda or seltzer
- 1 pound green beans, trimmed
- Coarse salt

Directions:

1. Line a plate with paper towels and set aside.
2. Place oil in a large pot so that it reaches a depth of 4 inches.
3. Heat over medium-high heat until oil reaches 350 degrees on a deep-fry thermometer.
4. Meanwhile, in a large bowl, whisk egg whites together until soft peaks form.
5. Whisk in flour and club soda.
6. Working in small batches, dip beans into batter, letting any excess drip off.
7. Carefully lower beans into oil. Cook, stirring periodically to keep beans from sticking together, until light golden brown, about 3 minutes.
8. Remove beans from oil using a slotted spoon and transfer to the paper towel-lined plate; season with salt.
9. Let oil return to 350 degrees on the deep-fry thermometer and repeat process until all beans have been fried.
10. Serve beans immediately.

Green Beans
Vinaigrette

Ingredients:

- Coarse salt and ground pepper
- 1 1/2 pounds green beans, stem ends trimmed
- 1 shallot, halved lengthwise, thinly sliced
- 1/4 cup Lemon Vinaigrette

Directions:

1. Fill a medium bowl with ice water and set aside.
2. Set a steamer basket in a large saucepan with a lid.
3. Fill with enough salted water to come just below basket.
4. Bring to a boil.
5. Place green beans in basket, and reduce heat to a simmer.
6. Cover pan, steam until tender, 4 to 6 minutes.
7. Using tongs or a slotted spoon, transfer beans to ice water to stop cooking.
8. Drain and pat dry with paper towels.
9. Place on a serving platter. Top with shallot, and drizzle with vinaigrette.
10. Season with salt and pepper.

Green Beans

with Tomatoes, Olives, and Eggs

Prep Time: 10 mins   Total Time: 15 mins   Servings: 4

Ingredients:

- 1 pound green beans, trimmed
- 1/2 cup grape tomatoes, halved
- 1/2 cup Kalamata olives, pitted and halved
- 2 teaspoons extra-virgin olive oil
- 2 hard-cooked eggs, chopped
- Coarse salt and ground pepper
- Lemon wedges

Directions:

1. In a large pot of boiling salted water, cook beans until crisp-tender, 3 minutes.
2. Drain and rinse under cold water.
3. Halve beans and place in a bowl, add tomatoes, olives, oil, and eggs.
4. Season with salt and pepper.
5. Serve with lemon wedges.

A good pairing with Poached Chicken or Grilled Salmon.

Mustard Greens
and Onions

Prep Time: 5 mins   Total Time: 15 mins   Servings: 4

Ingredients:

- 2 tablespoons Ghee
- 1 medium onion, cut into 1/4-inch dice
- 2 pounds mustard greens, washed and cut into 3-inch pieces
- 1 teaspoon coarse salt
- 1/4 teaspoon freshly ground pepper
- 1 teaspoon freshly squeezed lemon juice

Directions:

1. In a large high-sided skillet, heat Ghee over medium-high heat.
2. Add diced onion, and sauté until translucent and beginning to brown, about 6 minutes.
3. Add the prepared mustard greens, and sprinkle with salt and pepper.
4. Toss until greens are just wilted, adding more greens as they will fit into the pan.
5. Toss with lemon juice just before serving.

Mustard Greens
and Sweet-Onion Sauté

Prep Time: 15 mins   Total Time: 15 mins   Servings: 4

Ingredients:

- 1 tablespoon olive oil
- 1 sweet onion (such as Vidalia), halved and thinly sliced
- Coarse salt and ground pepper
- 1 1/2 pounds mustard greens (2 bunches), stems removed, sliced 1 inch crosswise
- 2 teaspoons cider vinegar

Chef's Notes:

Mustard greens are very perishable and do not keep well in the refrigerator. Plan on using them within a couple of days of purchase.

Directions:

1. In a large skillet, heat oil over medium-high.
2. Add onion, season with salt and pepper.
3. Cook, stirring frequently, until onion is tender and golden, 6 to 8 minutes.
4. Add as many greens to skillet as will fit.
5. Season with salt and pepper.
6. Cook until wilted, tossing and adding more greens as room becomes available, 2 to 3 minutes.
7. Stir in vinegar.
8. Season with salt and pepper, and serve.

Sautéed Shrimp
with Arugula

Ingredients:

- 1 tablespoon extra-virgin olive oil
- 1 teaspoon extra-virgin olive oil
- 1 cup cherry or grape tomatoes
- 1 garlic clove, minced
- 1 pound large shrimp, peeled and deveined
- 4 ounces wild or baby arugula (4 cups)
- Coarse salt and ground pepper
- 1 tablespoon fresh lemon juice

Directions:

1. In a large skillet, heat oil over medium-high.
2. Add tomatoes and cook, stirring often, until they blister, about 2 minutes.
3. Add garlic and cook until fragrant, 30 seconds.
4. Add shrimp and cook, stirring often, until almost opaque throughout, about 4 minutes.
5. Add arugula, season with salt and pepper, and toss until wilted, 1 minute.
6. Add lemon juice and toss to combine.

Seared Salmon
with Oranges and Fennel

Ingredients:

- 2 navel oranges, peeled, and segmented, plus 2 tablespoons fresh orange juice
- 1 small fennel bulb (stalks removed), halved lengthwise, cored, and thinly sliced crosswise, fronds reserved for garnish (optional)
- 1/4 cup pitted green olives, halved
- 2 tablespoons fresh lemon juice
- 2 teaspoons olive oil
- Coarse salt and ground pepper
- 4 skinless salmon fillets (6 ounces each)

Directions:

1. In a medium bowl, combine orange segments and juice, fennel, olives, lemon juice with 1 teaspoon of oil.
2. Season with salt and pepper, and toss gently.
3. Set aside until you're ready to serve.
4. In a large nonstick skillet, heat remaining teaspoon of oil to a medium heat.
5. Add salmon to pan, flat side down.
6. Cook until browned, just about 3 minutes.
7. Turn salmon
8. Cook until opaque throughout, just 2 to 3 minutes.
9. Serve salmon and topped with the orange mixture
10. Garnish with fennel fronds for that extra flair.

Steamed Cod
and Mixed Green Peas

Prep Time: 15 mins   Total Time: 15 mins   Servings: 1

Ingredients:

- 6 large basil leaves
- 1 cod fillet (5 ounces; 1 ¼ inches thick)
- Coarse salt
- ¼ cup mixed sugar snap peas (halved)
- ¼ cup snow peas
- ¼ cup English peas (shelled)
- 1 radish, very thinly sliced
- Garnish with small basil leaves

VINAIGRETTE

- ¼ cup extra-virgin olive oil
- 3 tablespoons fresh lemon juice
- ½ teaspoon sugar
- Coarse salt
- 3 tablespoons chopped fresh basil

Chef's Notes:

Vinaigrette can be refrigerated for up to 3 days in an airtight container. For richer flavors, bring to room temperature before using.

Directions:

Make the vinaigrette

1. Combine oil, lemon juice, sugar and ½ teaspoon salt in a blender or food processor.
2. Add chopped basil, and pulse to combine.

Make the fish and peas:

1. Bring 1 inch of water to a boil in a medium saucepan.
2. Line steamer basket with basil leaves.
3. Place fish on top of basil, and season generously with salt.
4. Set basket in saucepan.
5. Steam, covered, for 3 minutes.
6. Add peas, and steam, covered, until fish is opaque throughout and peas are bright green and tender, about 3 minutes more.
7. Transfer fish and peas to a plate using a spatula.
8. Top with radish, and drizzle with some vinaigrette.
9. Season with salt.
10. Garnish with small basil leaves.

Tilapia

with Arugula, Capers, and Tomatoes

Prep Time: 15 mins   Total Time: 15 mins   Servings: 1

Ingredients:

- ½ cup cherry tomatoes, halved
- ¼ teaspoon red-pepper flakes
- 1 tilapia filet (8 ounces)
- Coarse salt and ground pepper
- 2 small bunches arugula (about 3 cups)
- 1 tablespoon Ghee
- 1 tablespoon fresh lemon juice
- 1 tablespoon capers, rinsed and drained

Directions:

1. In a medium nonstick skillet, bring ¼ cup water to a boil.
2. Add tomatoes and red-pepper flakes, top with tilapia, and season with salt and pepper.
3. Cover, and cook 3 minutes.
4. Add arugula.
5. Cover, and cook until tilapia flakes easily with a fork, about 2 minutes.
6. With a slotted spoon, transfer tilapia and vegetables to a plate (reserve skillet).

Make sauce:

1. Off heat, add butter, lemon juice, and capers to skillet, swirl until Ghee has melted.
2. Season sauce with salt and pepper.
3. Serve tilapia over arugula and tomatoes, drizzle with sauce.

Grilled Zucchini
with Buttermilk-Basil Dressing

Prep Time: 5 mins   Total Time: 15 mins   Servings: 4

Ingredients:

- 5 tablespoons buttermilk
- 6 tablespoons extra-virgin olive oil
- 2 teaspoons white-wine vinegar
- 1 garlic clove, minced
- 1 cup packed fresh basil leaves
- 1/3 cup coarsely grated Parmesan
- Coarse salt and ground pepper
- 4 medium zucchini or yellow squash (or a combination), halved and cut lengthwise into 1/4-inch slices

Directions:

1. Heat a grill or grill pan over high.
2. Clean and lightly oil hot grill.
3. In a small measuring cup, combine buttermilk and 5 tablespoons extra-virgin olive oil with white-wine vinegar.
4. In a food processor, combine garlic, basil, and Parmesan and process until basil is finely chopped.
5. Season with salt and pepper. With machine running, add buttermilk mixture in a slow, steady stream and process until dressing is smooth.
6. Season to taste with salt and pepper.
7. Toss zucchini with remaining tablespoon oil.
8. Season with salt and pepper.
9. Grill zucchini (in batches if necessary) until lightly charred and tender, 4 to 6 minutes, flipping once.
10. Transfer to a serving plate and drizzle with dressing.

20 Minute Recipes

Cantaloupe, Prosciutto, and Arugula Salad

Sautéed Asparagus with Bacon

Baby Bok Choy with Ginger and Garlic

Brussels Sprouts with Vinegar-Glazed Red Onions

Sautéed Brussels sprouts With Raisins

Sautéed Brussels sprouts

Cauliflower Puree

Baked Ricotta and Greens Dip

Green Beans with Olives

Green Beans with Tapenade Dressing

Quick-Cooked Green Beans with Lemon

Bibb Lettuce Salad with Horseradish Dressing

Pork and Snap Pea Kebabs with Ginger-Hoisin Glaze

Roast Chicken with Lemons and Fennel

Cucumber and Smoked Salmon Sandwiches

Cucumber Salad with Salmon

Poached Salmon with Crushed Peas

Scallop Kebabs with Orange and Cucumber

Scallops and Brussels Sprouts

Scallops with Spinach and Arugula

Spicy Shrimp and Brussels Sprout Stir-Fry

Peas with Spinach and Bacon in Lettuce Cups

Snow Pea Salad with Shallot and Tarragon

Cauliflower Soup

Broiled Zucchini with Yogurt Sauce

Cantaloupe, Prosciutto
and Arugula Salad

Prep Time: 20 mins   Total Time: 20 mins   Servings: 6

Ingredients:

- 1/4 cup champagne vinegar or white-wine vinegar
- 1 tablespoon minced shallot
- 1/2 teaspoon minced garlic
- 1/2 teaspoon Dijon mustard
- 1/2 teaspoon salt, plus more to taste
- 1/4 teaspoon freshly ground black pepper, plus more to taste
- 1/2 cup vegetable oil or vegetable-olive oil blend
- 1 tablespoon minced mixed fresh herbs (basil, chives, and parsley)
- 8 ounces fresh arugula, rinsed and spun dry
- 1/2 cup thinly sliced red onion
- 1 cantaloupe, halved, seeded, peeled, and cut into thin wedges
- 6 to 8 thin slices prosciutto, torn into bite-size pieces

Directions:

1. In a mixing bowl, combine vinegar, shallot, garlic, mustard, salt, and pepper and whisk to combine.
2. While continuously whisking, add the oil in a slow, steady stream until completely incorporated.
3. Whisk in the herbs, and set aside while you prepare the salad.
4. In a large bowl, combine the arugula and red onion.
5. Drizzle in 1/4 cup of the vinaigrette and toss to combine.
6. Add more vinaigrette to taste.
7. Season with salt and pepper to taste.
8. Toss gently to combine.
9. Arrange the cantaloupe wedges on a large serving plate, top with the arugula salad and the prosciutto.
10. Serve immediately.

Have some extra vinaigrette? Refrigerate for up to 2 days in an airtight container.

Sautéed Asparagus
with Bacon

Prep Time: 5 mins   Total Time: 20 mins   Servings: 4

Ingredients:

- 2 slices bacon, cut into 1-inch pieces
- 2 bunches asparagus (2 pounds), trimmed and cut into 1-inch pieces
- Coarse salt and ground pepper
- 2 teaspoons Dijon mustard
- 3 tablespoons chopped fresh parsley

Directions:

1. In a large skillet, cook bacon over medium, stirring occasionally, until browned and crisp, 8 to 10 minutes.
2. With a slotted spoon, transfer to paper towels to drain.
3. Add asparagus to skillet and season with salt and pepper.
4. Cook, stirring, until asparagus is tender, about 10 minutes.
5. Remove from heat and stir in bacon, mustard, and parsley.

Baby Bok Choy
with Ginger and Garlic

Prep Time: 10 mins   Total Time: 20 mins   Servings: 6

Ingredients:

- 2 pounds baby bok choy (8 to 10), halved lengthwise and soaked in cold water to remove any dirt
- 2 teaspoons minced peeled fresh ginger
- 2 garlic cloves, thinly sliced
- 1 tablespoon plus 1 teaspoon toasted sesame oil
- 1/4 cup tamari soy sauce
- 2 tablespoons oyster sauce

Directions:

1. Bring a large pot of water to a boil.
2. Add bok choy (in two batches, if necessary), and cook until tender, 5 to 7 minutes.
3. Drain in a colander, let stand at least 5 minutes.
4. Transfer to a serving dish.
5. Meanwhile, cook ginger and garlic in oil in a small saucepan over medium-low heat, stirring, until ginger and garlic are soft, about 8 minutes.
6. Add tamari and oyster sauce, cook, stirring, until heated through, about 30 seconds more.
7. Pour sauce over bok choy, toss to coat.

Brussels sprouts

with Vinegar-Glazed Red Onions

Prep Time: 10 mins   Total Time: 20 mins   Servings: 4

Ingredients:

- 1 (about 10-ounce) Brussels sprouts
- Salt and freshly ground black pepper
- 1 tablespoon unsalted butter
- 1 tablespoon olive oil
- 1 small red onion, thinly sliced lengthwise
- 2 tablespoons balsamic vinegar

Directions:

1. Trim outer leaves and stems from Brussels sprouts, and discard.
2. Bring a medium pot of water to a boil, and add salt.
3. Meanwhile, prepare an ice-water bath.
4. Add Brussels sprouts to boiling water, and cook until tender but still bright green, about 4 minutes.
5. Remove from heat, drain, and plunge into ice-water bath to cool.
6. Drain well, and cut in half.
7. Heat 1/2 tablespoon butter and 1/2 tablespoon olive oil in a large heavy skillet over medium-high heat.
8. Add Brussels sprouts, and cook, tossing occasionally, until they are brown and crisp on the edges, about 3 minutes.
9. Season to taste with salt and pepper, and transfer to a large bowl.
10. Cover with aluminum foil to keep warm.
11. Add remaining 1/2 tablespoon each butter and oil to the same pan over medium-low heat.
12. Add onions, and cook, tossing occasionally, until wilted and transparent, about 3 to 4 minutes.
13. Add vinegar (stand back to avoid the fumes), and stir to loosen any brown bits on bottom of pan.
14. Cook until vinegar is reduced and the onions are glazed, about 30 seconds.
15. Add onions to Brussels sprouts, and toss well.
16. Serve immediately.

Sautéed Brussels sprouts
with Raisins

Prep Time: 5 mins   Total Time: 20 mins   Servings: 4

Ingredients:

- 1 tablespoon extra-virgin olive oil
- 10 ounces Brussels sprouts (about 25), stems trimmed, and thinly sliced
- 2 carrots, cut into 1/4-inch pieces (about 1/2 cup)
- 1/4 cup golden raisins
- 1 cup low-sodium canned chicken broth
- Coarse salt and freshly ground pepper

Chef's Notes:

Brussels sprouts are a member of the Gemmifera group of cabbages. High in Vitamin C and K as well as being high in Minerals like manganese, potassium, phosphorus and even omega-3 fatty acids, make Brussels sprouts a Remineralizing super food.

Directions:

1. Heat oil in a large skillet over medium heat.
2. Add Brussels sprouts and carrots.
3. Sauté until sprouts start to turn golden brown, about 3 minutes.
4. Add raisins and chicken broth.
5. Continue cooking, stirring occasionally, until sprouts are tender when pierced with a paring knife, about 12 minutes.
6. If the skillet becomes too dry before sprouts are tender, add up to 3 tablespoons water, and continue cooking.
7. Remove from heat, and season with salt and pepper.
8. Serve hot.

Sautéed
Brussels sprouts

Prep Time: 20 mins   Total Time: 20 mins   Servings: 8

Ingredients:

- 1/4 cup extra-virgin olive oil
- 2 pints Brussels sprouts (2 pounds total), trimmed and halved lengthwise
- Coarse salt and ground pepper
- 2 tablespoons fresh lemon juice

Directions:

1. In a large skillet, heat oil over medium-high.
2. Add Brussels sprouts, season with salt and pepper, and cook, stirring frequently, until caramelized, 8 to 10 minutes.
3. Add 1/3 cup water and cook until evaporated, about 2 minutes.
4. Add lemon juice and toss to coat.
5. Serve immediately.

Cauliflower
Purée

Prep Time: 5 mins   Total Time: 20 mins   Servings: 4

Ingredients:

- 1 Head cauliflower, stem and stalks trimmed, roughly chopped
- 1 Cup water or chicken stock
- 2 Tablespoons sour cream
- 1 Tablespoon unsalted butter, melt slightly
- Coarse salt and freshly ground pepper to taste

Chef's Notes:

If you don't have a food processor available, a hand blender will do the trick. Just blend until smooth.

Directions:

1. Combine cauliflower and water or chicken stock in a medium saucepan and bring to boil over high heat.
2. Reduce to a simmer, and cook until cauliflower is very tender, about 10 minutes.
3. With a slotted spoon, transfer cauliflower to the bowl of a food processor.
4. Add 2 tablespoons of cooking liquid. After about 20 seconds, add sour cream and butter.
5. Give it a spin for another 10 seconds and season with Salt and pepper to taste.
6. Make sure to serve it hot!

To add a simple garnish to this creamy side, just sauté a few cauliflower florets in a bit of oil or Ghee until golden brown.

Baked Ricotta
and Greens Dip

Ingredients:

- 1 cup ricotta
- 1 cup sautéed or steamed chopped greens (any greens you want)
- Crackers, etc., for serving

Directions:

1. Mix ricotta with greens in a shallow dish, season to taste.
2. Bake at 425 degrees until the top is light golden brown, about 12 minutes.
3. Serve the savory spread with crackers or just about anything.

Green Beans
with Olives

Prep Time: 15 mins   Total Time: 20 mins   Servings: 6

Ingredients:

- Coarse salt and ground pepper
- 1 1/2 pounds green beans, trimmed
- 1 jar (9 ounces) pimiento-stuffed olives, drained and rinsed
- 1 cup fresh parsley leaves
- 2 anchovy fillets
- 3 tablespoons extra-virgin olive oil
- 1 tablespoon red-wine vinegar

Directions:

1. In a large pot of boiling salted water, cook green beans until crisp-tender and bright green, about 6 minutes.
2. Drain and return to pot.
3. Meanwhile, in a food processor, pulse olives, parsley, anchovies, oil, and vinegar until olives are finely chopped.
4. Add to beans and stir to combine.
5. Season with pepper.
6. Serve at room temperature.

Chef's Notes:

Refrigerate for up to 1 day in an airtight container. After refrigeration, place the airtight container in warm water so that the dish can be served at room temperature.

Green Beans
with Tapenade Dressing

Prep Time: 20 mins   Total Time: 20 mins   Servings: 4

Ingredients:

- Coarse salt
- 1 pound green beans
- 1/4 cup black-olive tapenade
- 1 clove garlic, minced, or more to taste
- 1/2 cup coarsely chopped fresh flat-leaf parsley
- 2 teaspoons extra virgin olive oil
- Freshly ground pepper

Chef's Notes:

Fun Fact:

Cutting vegetables into strips lengthwise are called "Frenched".

Directions:

1. Bring a medium saucepan of salted water to a boil.
2. Plunge beans into boiling water, and cook until bright green and tender, 2 to 3 minutes.
3. Drain, and rinse in cold water to stop the cooking.
4. Trim the ends off the beans, and cut in half lengthwise.
5. Transfer beans to a serving bowl, and toss well with tapenade, garlic, parsley, and olive oil.
6. Season with salt and pepper.

Quick-Cooked Green Beans
with Lemon

Prep Time: 20 mins   Total Time: 20 mins   Servings: 4 to 6

Ingredients:

- 1 pound green beans, trimmed
- 2 tablespoons extra-virgin olive oil
- 4 cloves garlic, thinly sliced (2 tablespoons)
- Coarse salt and freshly ground pepper
- 1 small lemon, very thinly sliced (about 1/3 cup)

Directions:

1. Blanch green beans in a large pot of salted water until tender, 5 minutes.
2. Drain and transfer to a large plate or rimmed baking sheet to cool.
3. Heat oil in a large skillet over medium-high.
4. Add garlic and cook until softened and just beginning to color, 1 to 2 minutes.
5. Add green beans and season generously with salt and pepper.
6. When green beans are hot, toss in lemon slices and cook 1 minute over high.
7. Check seasoning -- beans should be well-seasoned and bright but not too sour.
8. Serve hot, or preferably at room temperature.

Bibb lettuce Salad
with Horseradish Dressing

Prep Time: 10 mins   Total Time: 20 mins   Servings: 4

Ingredients:

- 2 large eggs
- 2 tablespoons prepared horseradish
- 2 tablespoons champagne vinegar or white-wine vinegar
- 2 teaspoons honey
- 1 teaspoon Dijon mustard
- 1/2 teaspoon coarse salt
- 1/8 teaspoon freshly ground pepper
- 1/4 cup extra-virgin olive oil
- 2 large heads Bibb lettuce, torn into 1 1/2-inch pieces

Directions:

1. Place eggs in a small pot, and cover with cold water by 1 1/2 inches.
2. Bring to a boil, then remove from heat.
3. Cover, and let stand for 12 minutes.
4. Rinse with cold water, peel, and chop.
5. Combine horseradish, vinegar, honey, mustard, salt and pepper in a small bowl.
6. Add oil in a slow, steady stream, whisking until emulsified.
7. Arrange lettuce on a serving platter, sprinkle with chopped egg, and drizzle with vinaigrette.
8. Serve immediately.

Pork and Snap Pea Kebabs
with Ginger-Hoisin Glaze

Prep Time: 5 mins   Total Time: 20 mins   Servings: 4

Ingredients:

- 1/4 cup hoisin sauce
- 1 tablespoon soy sauce
- 1 tablespoon finely grated peeled fresh ginger (from a 1-inch piece)
- 1 tablespoon rice vinegar
- 1 pork tenderloin (about 3/4 pound), cut into 3/4-inch slices (Meatless option: 1 large eggplant, cut into 1-inch pieces.)
- 5 scallions, cut into 2-inch pieces
- 1/2 pound snap peas, trimmed

Directions:

1. Heat a grill to medium.
2. Clean and lightly oil hot grill.
3. In a small bowl, stir together hoisin sauce, soy sauce, ginger, and rice vinegar.
4. Alternately thread pork tenderloin, scallions, and snap peas onto four 8-inch skewers.
5. Grill, turning occasionally, until pork is cooked through and vegetables are charred, about 9 minutes.
6. Brush kebabs with hoisin mixture and cook 1 minute more, turning once, until mixture begins to bubble.

Chef's Notes:

You can also broil. Just set the rack to the second to the top. The recipes and cook time will be the same. Just make sure to us metal skewers.

Roast Chicken
with Lemons and Fennel

Prep Time: 5 mins   Total Time: 20 mins   Servings: 4

Ingredients:

- 1 chicken (3 1/2 to 4 pounds), rinsed and patted dry
- Pinch of Coarse salt and ground pepper
- 2 lemons, halved or quartered
- 3 fennel bulbs (2 1/2 pounds total), cored, stalks discarded, and cut into 1-inch wedges
- 1 tablespoon olive oil

Chef's Notes:

Chicken has a strict no pink rule! To insure your poultry is done, use a thermometer, at least 165 degrees in the thickest part of the thigh.

Directions:

1. Preheat oven to 400 degrees.
2. Place chicken on a large rimmed baking sheet
3. Season with salt and pepper.
4. Place a lemon half in cavity.
5. Using kitchen twine, tie legs together.
6. Add fennel and remaining lemons to sheet and toss with oil.
7. Roast chicken until thermometer inserted into thickest part of a thigh registers 165 degrees, 60 to 70 minutes.
8. Baste chicken with pan juices every 15 to 20 minutes.
9. Toss fennel about 30 minutes in.
10. Transfer chicken to a platter and cover with foil.
11. Let rest 10 minutes.
12. Carve chicken.
13. Serve with fennel and lemons.

Cucumber Sandwiches
with Smoked Salmon

Prep Time: 5 mins   Total Time: 20 mins   Servings: 20-25 sandwiches

Ingredients:

- 1/4 pound smoked salmon, finely chopped
- 2 tablespoons finely chopped red onion
- 2 teaspoons finely chopped fresh cilantro
- 1 jalapeno chili, seeded and finely chopped
- Finely grated zest of 1 lime
- Coarse salt and freshly ground pepper
- 1 English cucumber
- 1/4 cup crème fraiche, well chilled
- 1 lime, peeled and segmented, each segment cut into 4 pieces

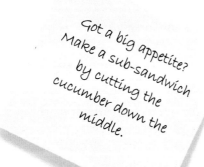

Got a big appetite? Make a sub-sandwich by cutting the cucumber down the middle.

Directions:

1. Make tartare: In a small bowl, combine salmon, onion, cilantro, jalapeno and zest. Season with salt and pepper to taste.
2. Using a paring knife or vegetable peeler, remove skin on two opposite sides of cucumber. Trim the ends, cut cucumber crosswise into 40 to 50 slices, 1/4 inch thick.
3. Place slices on paper towels to dry.
4. Using a butter knife or a small offset spatula, spread about 1/2 teaspoon of crème fraiche on half of the cucumber slices, and top with a teaspoon of tartare.
5. Place remaining cucumber slices on top, followed by a small dollop of crème fraiche and a piece of lime.
6. Serve immediately or cover with plastic wrap and chill for up to 1 hour.

Consuming raw or undercooked meats, poultry, seafood, shellfish, or eggs may increase your risk of foodborne illness.

Cucumber Salad
with Salmon

Prep Time: 5 mins   Total Time: 20 mins   Servings: 4

Ingredients:

- 3/4 pound skinless salmon fillet
- Pinch of Coarse salt and ground pepper
- 1 tablespoon sherry vinegar
- 1 tablespoon olive oil
- 1 teaspoon honey
- 1/2 Vidalia onion
- 1/2 seedless cucumber
- 1 tablespoon nonpareil or very small capers

Directions:

1. Preheat oven to 450 degrees.
2. Place salmon on a rimmed baking sheet, season with salt and pepper.
3. Bake until opaque throughout, 10 to 13 minutes. Using a fork, gently flake fish into bite-size pieces
4. Let cool to room temperature.
5. In a medium bowl, whisk together vinegar, oil and honey.
6. Season with salt and pepper.
7. Add salmon, onion, cucumber and capers
8. Toss to combine.
9. Serve immediately, or refrigerate for up to 4 hours.

Not a fan of Sherry Vinegar? Replace with Red-wine Vinegar and add a little more honey to the dressing.

Poached Salmon
with Crushed Peas

Prep Time: 10 mins   Total Time: 20 mins   Servings: 4

Ingredients:

- 4 skinless salmon fillets (5 ounces each, about 1 inch thick)
- 1 leek, halved and rinsed well
- 1/2 teaspoon whole peppercorns, plus freshly ground pepper
- Coarse salt
- 2 tablespoons thinly sliced basil leaves, plus sprigs for garnish
- 1 teaspoon finely grated lemon zest and 1/4 cup lemon juice (from 2 lemons)
- 1/2 teaspoon sugar
- 1/3 cup extra-virgin olive oil
- 2 cups shelled fresh garden peas (from 2 pounds in pods)
- 1 tablespoon thinly sliced fresh mint leaves

Salmon are anadromous, they are born in fresh water, migrate to salt water, then return to freshwater to spawn.

Directions:

1. Place salmon in a pot, add leek, peppercorns, 2 teaspoons salt and 4 cups water.
2. Bring to just under a boil, reduce heat and cook at a simmer until salmon is cooked through, 4 to 5 minutes. Remove from water and cover to keep moist.
3. Puree sliced basil and lemon zest in a food processor. Add sugar and lemon juice while pulsating to make a vinaigrette. With machine running, add oil and season with salt to taste.
4. Bring a medium pot of water to a boil.
5. Add 1 tablespoon salt and the peas. Reduce heat, and vigorously simmer until tender and bright green, about 4 minutes.
6. Drain, and transfer to a bowl.
7. Add 2 tablespoons basil vinaigrette, and crush with a potato masher.
8. Season with salt and pepper, then add mint.
9. Divide peas among 4 plates, and top with salmon. Drizzle with more vinaigrette, and garnish with basil sprigs.

Scallop Kebabs

with Orange and Cucumber

Prep Time: 20 mins   Total Time: 20 mins   Servings: 4

Ingredients:

- Olive oil, for grates
- 2 tablespoons honey
- 1/2 navel orange, halved and cut into 1/2-inch wedges
- 1/4 cup fresh orange juice
- 1/4 cup orange juice
- 8 very thin slices peeled fresh ginger
- 1/2 Kirby cucumber, halved lengthwise and cut into 1/2-inch slices
- 1 pound large scallops
- Coarse salt and ground pepper

Directions:

1. Heat grill to medium
2. Clean and lightly oil hot grates.
3. In a small bowl, combine honey and orange juice.
4. Onto four skewers, thread orange wedges (through skin), ginger, cucumber and scallops, beginning and ending with orange wedges.
5. Season with salt and pepper.
6. Grill kebabs until scallops are opaque throughout, 4 to 6 minutes
7. Turn and baste with honey mixture halfway through.

Chef's Notes:

If using wooden skewers, make sure to soak in water for 30 minutes before use.

Scallops
and Brussels Sprouts

Prep Time: 5 mins   Total Time: 20 mins   Servings: 4

Ingredients:

- 4 large scallops
- 4 tablespoons Ghee
- Coarse salt and freshly ground pepper
- 12 Brussels sprouts, trimmed, leaves separated
- 4 tablespoons Jalapeno Dressing
- 1/4 red onion, finely chopped
- 1/4 cup cilantro leaves
- 1 jalapeno, half of the seeds discarded, finely chopped

Directions:

1. Heat 2 tablespoons clarified butter or Ghee, on medium-high in a medium skillet.
2. Season scallops with salt and pepper
3. Add to pan and cook, turning once, until golden brown, 2 to 3 minutes per side.
4. In another medium skillet, heat remaining 2 tablespoons clarified butter or ghee over medium heat.
5. Add Brussels sprouts to skillet and season with salt and pepper.
6. Cook until slightly crisp, 30 to 45 seconds.
7. Toss Brussels sprouts with 2 tablespoons jalapeno dressing until coated. Place on a serving plate; top with scallops.
8. In a small bowl, mix together onion, cilantro, and jalapeno with remaining 2 tablespoons jalapeno dressing.
9. Spoon over scallops and serve immediately.

Scallops

with Spinach and Arugula

Prep Time: 10 mins   Total Time: 20 mins   Servings: 4

Ingredients:

- 16 large trimmed sea scallops, rinsed and dried
- 1 1/2 teaspoons coarse salt
- 1/4 teaspoon freshly ground pepper
- 3 tablespoons safflower oil
- 2 garlic cloves, thinly sliced lengthwise
- 7 ounces baby spinach
- 7 ounces baby arugula
- 1/4 teaspoon crushed red-pepper flakes

Though scallops cook very quickly, the trick is to get a good sear on it with hot oil that is not so hot its smoking.

Directions:

1. Heat a large straight-sided skillet over medium-high heat.
2. Sprinkle scallops with 1 teaspoon salt and 1/8 teaspoon pepper.
3. Heat 2 tablespoons oil in skillet.
4. Arrange scallops in skillet, and cook on 1 side until golden brown, about 7 minutes. Flip, and cook until scallops are opaque, 45 to 60 seconds.
5. Transfer to a plate lined with paper towels or coffee filters.
6. Reduce heat to medium, and add remaining tablespoon oil to skillet.
7. Add garlic, and cook for 15 seconds.
8. Add spinach, arugula, red-pepper flakes, and remaining 1/2 teaspoon salt and 1/8 teaspoon pepper.
9. Cook, tossing greens often, until just wilted, about 2 minutes.
10. Transfer to a platter, top with scallops, and serve immediately.

Spicy Shrimp
and Brussels Sprout Stir-Fry

Prep Time: 20 mins   Total Time: 20 mins   Servings: 4

Ingredients:

- 2 tablespoons vegetable oil, divided
- 1 pound Brussels sprouts, trimmed and shredded
- Salt and pepper
- 1 cup bean sprouts
- 2 cloves garlic, thinly sliced
- 1 small green chili, thinly sliced
- 3 scallions, white and green parts separated and thinly sliced
- 1 pound medium shrimp (43 to 52), peeled and deveined (tails on or off, your chose)
- 2 teaspoons toasted sesame oil
- Lime wedges, for serving

Chef's Notes:

Use a food processor to make fast work of shredding the Brussels sprouts. No processor, no problem, just use a sharp knife and your mad ninja skills to get the job done.

Directions:

1. In a large skillet or wok, heat 1 tablespoon vegetable oil over medium-high.
2. In 2 batches, sauté Brussels sprouts until tender, about 5 minutes.
3. Season with salt and pepper.
4. Put Brussels on a platter.
5. Add bean sprouts to pan and cook until heated through, roughly 1 minute
6. Add to platter.
7. Wipe out pan, add remaining tablespoon vegetable oil, and return to heat.
8. Add garlic, chili, and scallion whites and cook until fragrant, 30 to 40 seconds.
9. Add shrimp, season with salt and pepper, and sauté until opaque throughout, 4 to 6 minutes.
10. Add to platter, drizzle with sesame oil, top with scallion greens, and toss.
11. Serve with lime wedges.

Peas and Spinach

with Bacon in Lettuce Cups

Prep Time: 10 mins   Total Time: 20 mins   Servings: 6

Ingredients:

- 4 slices bacon, cut into 1/2-inch pieces
- 2 tablespoons Ghee
- 2 leeks (white and pale-green parts only), halved, thinly sliced into half-moons, and rinsed well (2 cups)
- Coarse salt and freshly ground pepper
- 20 ounces spinach, tough stems removed, washed well (8 packed cups)
- 2 cups shelled fresh garden peas (from 2 pounds in pods)
- 1/2 cup chicken broth
- 1 tablespoon finely chopped mixed fresh herbs, such as dill, chervil, and tarragon
- 12 leaves Boston or Bibb lettuce

Directions:

1. Cook bacon in a skillet over medium heat until crisp, about 10 minutes.
2. Transfer to a paper-towel-lined plate to drain.
3. Melt Ghee in a large pot over medium-high heat
4. Add leeks and 1 teaspoon salt.
5. Cook, stirring occasionally, until leeks are translucent, about 3 minutes.
6. Add spinach, cover, and cook 2 minutes, stirring halfway through.
7. Add peas and broth, and cook, stirring occasionally, until peas are tender and bright green, 3 to 4 minutes.
8. Stir in herbs and bacon, and season with salt and pepper.
9. Divide lettuce leaves among 6 plates, and top with pea mixture.
10. Serve immediately.

Snow Pea Salad

with Shallot and Tarragon

Prep Time: 20 mins   Total Time: 20 mins   Servings: 4

Ingredients:

- 2 teaspoons Dijon mustard
- 2 tablespoons champagne or white-wine vinegar
- 1/4 cup extra-virgin olive oil
- Salt and pepper
- 2 tablespoons minced shallot
- 1 pound snow peas, thinly sliced lengthwise
- 2 tablespoons chopped fresh tarragon

Directions:

1. In a large bowl, whisk together mustard, vinegar, and oil.
2. Season with salt and pepper.
3. Add shallot, snow peas, and tarragon and combine.

Cauliflower
Soup

Prep Time: 15 mins   Total Time: 20 mins   Servings: 4

Ingredients:

- 3 tablespoons olive oil, plus more for frying
- 1 large head cauliflower, trimmed, halved, and cut into 1/4-inch slices (7 to 8 cups)
- 1 shallot, thinly sliced
- 5 to 6 cups Homemade Vegetable Stock, heated through
- Coarse salt and pepper, to taste
- 1 cup 1/4-inch cubes brioche bread
- Fresh flat-leaf parsley leaves, for garnish

Directions:

1. In a large skillet, heat 3 tablespoons olive oil over medium-high heat.
2. Add cauliflower and shallot.
3. Cook, stirring occasionally, until cauliflower begins to lightly brown and is completely softened, 10 to 12 minutes.
4. Working in batches, transfer cauliflower and shallot to the jar of a blender.
5. Add enough of the heated stock to easily blend and process until smooth.
6. Pass through a fine mesh sieve or chinois and transfer to a medium saucepan.
7. Bring to a simmer over medium heat.
8. Season with salt and pepper.
9. Cook until heated through.
10. Fill a small skillet 1/4 inch high with olive oil.
11. Heat over medium heat.
12. Add bread cubes and cook, stirring frequently, until bread is toasted.
13. Transfer to a paper towel-lined plate to drain.
14. Season with salt and pepper.
15. Add parsley leaves to skillet and cook until crisp.
16. Transfer to a paper towel-lined plate to drain.
17. Divide soup evenly between 4 bowls.
18. Top with toasted bread cubes and fried parsley leaves.
19. Serve.

Broiled Zucchini
with Yogurt Sauce

Ingredients:

- 2 tablespoons extra-virgin olive oil
- 4 medium zucchini, halved lengthwise
- Coarse salt and ground pepper
- 1/3 cup low-fat plain yogurt
- 1 tablespoon lemon juice
- 1/4 teaspoon ground coriander
- 1/4 teaspoon ground mustard
- 1/4 cup fresh cilantro leaves

Directions:

1. Heat broiler. Brush a rimmed baking sheet with 1 tablespoon oil.
2. Arrange zucchini in a single layer, cut side up.
3. Brush with 1 tablespoon oil and season with salt and pepper.
4. Broil until zucchini are deep golden brown, 8 to 10 minutes.
5. Meanwhile, in a small bowl, stir together yogurt, lemon juice, coriander, and mustard.
6. Season with salt and pepper.
7. Transfer zucchini to a serving platter, drizzle with yogurt sauce, and sprinkle with cilantro.

Index

Made in the USA
Las Vegas, NV
27 February 2022